The Lesser Light

Volume I

poems by

Philip Wexler

Finishing Line Press
Georgetown, Kentucky

The Lesser Light

Volume I

Publisher: Leah Huete de Maines

Editor: Christen Kincaid

Front Cover Art: *Still Life with Vase, Corn and Moon*—Philip Wexler,
November 2018, Glass Mosaic

Interior Photo: GettyIStockImages

Back Cover Art: *Rising Moon Over Mount Nanping: Cao Cao*
from the series One Hundred Aspects of the Moon by Tsukioka Yoshitoshi,
1885. Used with permission from Irwin Lavenberg, Lavenberg Collection of
Japanese Prints

Author Photo: Philip Wexler

Cover Design: Elizabeth Maines McCleavy

Order online: www.finishinglinepress.com
also available on amazon.com

Author inquiries and mail orders:
Finishing Line Press
P. O. Box 1626
Georgetown, Kentucky 40324
U. S. A.

For Planet Earth

That it May Be Repaired and Restored,
Flourish Anew
and Prosper in Peace
under the Greater and Lesser Lights

"And God said, 'Let there be lights in the firmament of the heaven to divide the day from the night: and let them be for signs, and for seasons, and for days, and for years'...And God made two great lights; the greater light to rule the day, and **the lesser light** to rule the night...And God set them in the firmament of heaven to give light upon the earth. And to rule over the day and over the night, and to divide the light from the darkness: and God saw that it was good."

—Genesis 1 (King James Version)

Foreword

The Lesser Light is a sequence of poems about the moon I began many years ago. It was originally suggested to me by the Japanese artist Tsukioka Yoshitoshi's *100 Views of the Moon* (1) woodblock print series. The prints inspired me to write 100 poems that evoked the moon or resonated with moonness. My aim was *not* to write a poem to match each of the prints, which deal largely with Japanese history and mythology (although a few touch upon this subject), but to try to distill something of the moon's indefinable essence in my reaction to its myriad manifestations.

Having spent a few years completing the 100 poems, I titled the manuscript, *100 Views of the Moon*, in homage to Yoshitoshi (1839-1892). I assumed the project was complete but didn't realize how insistent the urging of the moon could be. I didn't particularly have publication in mind at the outset but as the collection grew, I thought, *why not?*

After completing poem number 200, I titled the new manuscript *200 Views of the Moon*. By the time I reached 300, a better title was in order—thus, the biblically derived, *The Lesser Light*, which I have retained now through the completion of over 1000 moon poems, many still in rough draft. I have selected, edited, and experimented with assorted rearrangements to arrive at this 500-poem sequence, designated Volume I. It seems likely that I will continue to write additional moon poems and tinker with existing ones. It troubles me only a bit that I should find so overdone a poetic subject so compelling. I am not out to break any records but see no reason to self-impose a stopping point and will quit when the mood (to write) fails to strike me. For all I know, some ancient poet may have written 10,000 poems about the moon, or maybe 10,000 poets have. One can still be optimistic that there is enough of this *lesser* light to go around for the foreseeable future.

(1) Lately, *100 Aspects of the Moon* seems to be the preferred English language translation of the Yoshitoshi series. Not knowing Japanese, I cannot comment on the accuracy of *aspects* over *views*, but it seems to me perhaps a more apt descriptor since *views*, while not restricted to the visual, is more suggestive of it, while *aspects* encompasses a broader range—imagery, culture, history, folklore, etc.

1

which is whiter?
the moon or the snow
it illuminates?
which is more pure—
white or bluish
white?

2

the smitten oarsman rowed
at her command. she stood
at the bow in a sheer billowing
nightgown, eyes to the sky,
singing as if she were the ocean
swelling at high tide.

3

i dreamt the sun
came out at night,
the moon in the day.
on the beach
in the afternoon
her tan was white
and chalky.

4

raindrops tenuously
hanging from the armrest
of a wrought iron chair
prompt me to grab
at the purple night
for deliverance.

5

in the rodeo of the heavens,
he whirls and whips a lasso far

to catch an unwary moon.
earthbound on a pier,
his double casts a line
to where the moon used to be
and reels in a bucking shadow.

6

in this dry place,
my mind reverts
to the lunar
crater of boredom,
where i trek alone,
kicking and kicking but
not a spark.

7

moon pours almond light
over ghostly prairie.

8

observe the moon's phases
and moods. meditate
on its passage through
the cycle, past and future.
take stock of your present.

9

i thought i could find
safe harbor somewhere
on this planet
but am so haunted
by everything destined
never to happen.

10

late afternoon.
two gray squirrels spiral
up sycamore and out
to branch's pliant tip,
rock up and down, feast
on walnuts and focus
on an inconspicuous patch
of sky as the invisible
takes shape.

11

the moon is a goblet.
Ishimoto drinks almond milk
on the temple steps.
his intended watches him
from the water.
he has emptied many goblets
since he lost her there.

12

at such times
when my cheek fits
neatly into the curve
of the moon,
i need neither
anyone's company
nor my own.

13

when the concert let out
and my ears played back
the tender wail of trumpet,
my eyes were pulled up
by the harmonic
tone of gravity.

14

nightly, she'd reflect
on her naked body
in the full-length mirror
alongside the window.
one time, she kept gazing
long past dark but
it never grew dim.

15

he is on a horse knee-deep in water,
in full armor, red plated, a spear
at his side, feet lightly planted
in stirrups. he peers intently
at a hut across the lake, darkening
like the sky. he is expecting
someone or something to emerge.
up above, a full moon
is struggling to be reborn.

16

sheep graze on moon grass.
science has made great strides.

17

i saw you orange last night.
i know you are a woman.
teach me how to love you.
i know you make love.
i saw you orange last night.

18

up high, the pregnant moon
once more wonders how
it will nurse its young.

again, it will turn
slim before the birth.

19

the room is bright.
close your eyes before
you hit the light switch.
when lights go out
you'll see a succession
of deep green moons
fading, just one step
ahead of you
down the same deep tunnel.
now try shutting
the lights off first.
see the difference?

20

it rips through me,
this news you carry
over our beers.
i will get no sleep.
i wish you had waited
till dawn.

21

that Halloween,
we tired of pumpkins
bereft of inner light,
perpetually seeking
candles. instead,
we carved the moon.

22

abashedly looking at my feet,
i pleaded with the moon

to tell me if i was making
a mistake by choosing
the girl with the jet-black eyes.
when i lifted my head
the answer was spelled out
in the clouds drifting across its face.

23

you cannot fathom the labor of my rising.
from your vantage, it must seem easy.
but don't be mistaken—i need prodding.
i am as little inclined to wake up
at dusk as you are in the morning
and these night hours are a drain.
i shun makeup but keep a bright face,
letting light work for me, and have been told
i am alluring partially hidden behind mist.
believe me, it takes practice. i don't deny
i am changeable but aren't we all?

24

horses cavorting
in the black golf course
at midnight
disturb
the green lawns
of strategy.

25

the sunlit sky is already soaking in
through the east facing window
but your sleepiness is fixated
on a period not long past.
hovering between your eyes
are reminders of deep nocturnal hours.

26

in a long silver gown,
hand in hand with
a dark-complexioned dancer,
you swirl around each other
until he fades,
leaving you to spin
on your own axis.

27

but they,
poor souls,
walk white
with the transmutation
of the moon.

28

crickets and fireflies.
ears and eyes strain
for signs of summer
along earth's edges.
then suddenly you look up.

29

teapot on windowsill.
midnight blue glaze
catches white
satellite reflection.

30

what need for that
distant inert ball
and its fickle cycles
when at the flick

of a switch we have
dependable streetlamps?

31

a stallion runs,
has wild eyes,
eats the moon.
his mare gives birth
to wild moons.

32

in the dark silence of the sky
where we risk misdirection,
we are guided by a silver buzz.

33

empty handed, she flies
into the middle of the night.
i envy her. she needs no baggage.

34

take a good look
at your fingernails
and you'll know
what i'm talking about.

35

hot Spanish music and sweating August
night air invade my rumpled apartment.
for a moment, a moderating breeze
from the window calms my fevered chills.
something snaps. the Venetian blinds
drop down like a guillotine chopping off
my rebel thoughts.

36

i guess i didn't look
where i was going
when i strolled down
the puddled ghetto street
for i stopped just short
of stepping on the moon.

37

who would ever give me a pass
if i confessed i masturbated
while salivating over pictures
in astronomy books?

38

i am intrigued by glimmers
of romance peering out
between fitfully moving clouds.

39

dandelion encased in
acrylic paperweight.
straw yellow center
shoots out frozen
sprays of white silk.
is it like that up there?
weightless splashing
fixed forever?

40

she tried to reassure us both saying,
"fortunately, the moon has no ears
for we say such wicked things
to each other." "no ears," i parried,
but it overhears our every word."

41

surface area of Africa,
gravity one sixth of Earth,
mass one eightieth or so,
can't hold atmosphere,
light rough highlands,
dark smooth seas,
idyllic—from a distance.

42

the hour grew late, the conference
interminable and vision blurry
but breakdown was averted
by a reverberating gong
rattling the building—a psyche-
saving missive from the moon.

43

pink, feathery clouds
tickle moon's neck.
i feel myself swept up
in the embrace.

44

you lovers make of me
more than i am. go ahead,
send me your vain wishes.
it's a harmless game.
should a stray one comes true,
i'll take credit. as for the rest,
please look elsewhere to pin blame.

45

there now, you've shut the window
on the moon's delicate fingers.
i can't abide this clumsiness. do be

careful, Henry, before you plunge
us all into hostile darkness.

46

after weeks of steady rain,
lightning hits the valley
and the moon, abruptly, sprouts.

47

when you scratch my back
i contemplate
the far side of the moon.

48

on the picnic blanket,
you lie on your back.
i touch your forehead.
the moon looks down
on you looking up at me.
yes, I have decided—
i want what you want.

49

we're agreed it's only once
a month the moon is full
but the nights before and after
come close to fooling us
with too little or too much,
making for friendly arguments.

50

Takana stalked his enemy many years.
A fatal thrust cleanly pierced the heart.
the bloodied blade came out the back,
its vengeful tip pointing up to the moon.

51

our carefulness in
fording the creek.
this is how we would
step on the moon.

52

in the field where
there are no lights,
we plot our crimes
mistakenly thinking
no one watches.

53

the moon on crutches, winded,
having a hard time even
making it through midnight,
disillusioned by the apathy
below. not even a blown kiss.

54

not space behind the moon,
but a hole it has bandaged.
nor space inside the hole,
but the face of destiny.

55

police out with hounds
and flashlights through
wooded tangle where
kidnapper ever desperate
for final escape runs,
clutching gagged child
like bag of potatoes
in his tattooed arms.

56

in the speeding commuter train
your eyes glom onto the newspaper
until a jolting brake, and blackout
urges shift of attention from lap to
suddenly nonreflective window
where you see the frightful moon
full and striped by atmospheric
threads of white and grey.

57

your billions of eyes upon me,
i try so hard to be humble
but cannot help shining.

58

red and gold streamers,
they fly with the speeding
'57 Chevy Corvair
to honeymoon destinations
intended and unanticipated.

59

you are the clock
that precedes all clocks,
yet will keep ticking
once the rest are stilled.
we measure time in secret,
where punctuality is assured.

60

with Vegas behind me,
i tore through the roads
to reach the Utah canyons,
my mouth agape at wonders

that trivialized the meaningless
winnings in my pocket.

61

long after zoo closing
and crowds depart,
glistening seals climb
on their favorite rocks
and gaze longingly
at the sky.

62

i and my drunken friends
spent many a night debating
which direction it would go
if we pissed on the moon.

63

nightly, sirens
howl through the city.
municipal police
patrol the streets
while we keep watch
for galactic disturbances.

64

i am alone in a room
void of color.
the curtains are drawn
and the door locked.
how comes this
ancient orb here?

65

a breast exposed
in the subway car.

a baby suckles
the moon.

66

not with eyes alone,
but also heart.
more piercing
than the flame's orange,
its veins of blue. lessons
less of quenching
than of thirst.

67

white headed crow picking
at the grass among his
steel black cousins—
born from the mating
of moon with night.

68

Hector, sweetheart,

i know you miss us
as we miss you.
it's been so long.
i still can't believe
you forgot to pack
the white mohair
sweater i knitted
for your birthday.
i'm wearing it now.
remember, ages ago,
when we used to look
up together? i swear
i can pinpoint you.
it's two years already.
i hope you will send
for us soon.

regards to Captain Wallace.

your own, Adella

69

Adella, querida mia

life up here
is lonely and barren
without you. still,
the place has potential.
sorry about the delay
but the station's
enlargement is almost
complete and we are
making arrangements
for your and Paulito's
arrival. i am enclosing
a little rock for him.
we'll be together
before you know it,
like a pioneer family
having gone, instead
of out West, simply out.

besos y abrazos, Hector

70

dear Dad,

thanks for your letter
and the meteor fragment.
Mom and I miss you a lot
and cry sometimes when
we think about you.
everybody at school
says you're super,
and wants to come along
when you send for us.

i hope it will be soon.
can I bring my bike?
how do frisbees fly there?

love, Paulito

71

dear Mrs. Consuelo,

times have been difficult.
i must in all honesty
tell you that Mr. Consuelo
has fallen under the spell
of the moon maidens.
long ago he gave up any
thought of having you
join him. he worships
the seductive creatures.
i've been tempted myself.
don't be taken in by his letters.
security dictates our screening them.
take my advice and make
a new future for yourself.
Mr. Consuelo is as if drugged,
does not sleep, and dreams awake.

my sincere regrets, Captain Wallace

72

through the tropical windshield
steaming with equatorial lust,
the laser brightness of the moon
burns cool on your temples.

73

one night,
sky and trees
equally black.

walking down
the rocky path
you could
be blindfolded.
two weeks later,
visible sky cleaves
the dark branches,
funnels down to
your grateful eyes—
heavenly progress.

74

it is the fruit that grows
on the tree of night.
admirers graze on these
upper reaches and all
share the same ripe pick.

75

now Jonathan, if you don't
eat all your peas
you'll be sent straight
to bed without moon
for dessert. and just let me
catch you trying to draw
that curtain open and you'll be
served peas all week.

76

under the bridge—
tender banter
and all-out love
transition to glimmering
reflections in water.
there is no distinguishing
one light from the next
when so immersed.

77

crickets in July.
we are thankful for the chirps
muffling our amorous murmurs
as we share soft churchyard grass
with the dead, bringing them
remembrance of their late joys.

78

between live oak branches
bearing moss at
bayou's living end
are dark and shining volumes
as much Louisiana as
the boggy soil i stand in.

79

the moon is a nickel
the waitress forgot
to pick up
from the last customer.
Monticello
is the moon,
Thomas Jefferson—
the man inside.

80

penned up in this jail cell
these last five years
i've done nothing
but write about the moon
without even once glancing
up to see if it was there.
but keep in mind
that it took thirty years
of mute admiration before

i was brave enough
to lift my pen.

81

i dared hope you'd hear
my serenade vining up
the trellis but see
no sign. are you listening?
once more, i sing
for no one. how can i
ever convince you i exist?

82

sparsely vegetated dunes
welcome haggard travelers
disdainful of the remoteness
but desperate, before
they collapse, for any
open stretch to dig in.

83

your sprightly step—
i know none lighter.
did you pick it up
from your days
in the dancing circle
or your voyage outside
the circumference?

84

we've grown so sick
of daylight. we understand
why you took offense but
haven't we apologized
enough? it's been an eternity.
please come back.

85

my dachshund plays
with dirty white socks.
this evening i will
pet him with one hand
and paint the moon
with the other.

86

icicles on pine needles
harbor circles of light.
outer space turns inner.
we learn about ourselves
by exploring elsewhere.

87

too hot for him to sleep.
leaning out the window
with a restless smoke,
he feels caged behind
the fire escape.
through its bars he scans
the red neon glow
of the "Cocktail Lounge"
where he first met
the half-naked woman
sprawled on his bed.

88

weather forecast for
the moon today—
same as usual,
zero chance of rain,
humidity—zilch,
sunny and brutally hot
on one side, dark

and frigidly cold
on the other.

89

that daybreak of despair
when i didn't know
where to turn,
i was befriended
by an ellipse.

90

our wisdom, not earthbound
but fragile as ever.
owl screeches to moon
in language of desire.
moon obliges with a stream
of ghostly rodents.

91

i suffered through dark
fiery shrieks exploding
around the edge.
when you came between me
and the sun, my hair
stood on end.

92

a fair exchange—
i surrender my knight
to gain your bishop.
this game, now
more than a game,
funnels into morning.
all of us—pawns
in a grand stalemate.

93

dawn creeps up.
caterpillar in the milkweed
squiggling high, low,
goodbye, hello.
slowly the moon
retraces its steps.

94

a pat of cream cheese
on burnt toast.
i am alert to
likenesses of places
i've seen
but never been.

95

no wonder she was shivering in the trash
and cat strewn alley, trying to make
a living in her red vinyl microskirt.
she bumped up against me, asked
if i'd like some company, pointed
to a room at the top of the rundown
boarding house, and touted the view
as awesome. "above or below?"
i wondered aloud. "either way,
a damn sight better than the street."
she smiled broadly, unconcerned
about letting me see a chipped front tooth.
a cat screeched. she tucked her arm
in mine. i did not resist.

96

you are the bright gloss
lining the moon's dark edge.
i reach for you

with my eyes.
when my eyes close,
i reach beyond.

97

the curtains are a sliver
apart. the family says
their prayers and peeks out
at something peeking in.

98

you know the moon is
no more than a giant
reflector for the sun.
as lamplight thrown
by a mirror
is still lamplight,
so moonlight is
only sunlight.

99

go ahead, moon, finish
your story. i am awake.
tell me where
you will gravitate
when time slows down.
let me stay near you.
tell me the ending
before i run out
of time.

100

turtles grow sleepy
at odd hours.

101

tourists marvel at the Capitol
Dome, the Taj Mahal's,
St. Peter's, and the like.
so they should, but now
and then, look higher.

102

taunting me
with its crusty white
sneer of mountains,
and craters, i am not
intimidated by this
devil of a moon. watch me
grimace in return.

103

the cult
of chrome
doorknobs
holds services
in the junkyard
as sunrise
makes its entrance
and rats
scurry away.

104

the moon
is a Chinese dumpling.
as a boy, i plucked it
out of the dark stew
of space with solid silver
chopsticks, and chewed
slowly. even now,
i savor that taste.

105

according to schedule
and gradation, the moon
frowns at my being
wholly or partly conspicuous,
but only celebrates as i dwindle
into total darkness.

106

people assume my son,
Jacob, is intrigued
by the moon since
he says the word
so often. to me,
it's simply his version
of the sound he heard
the cow make
that sweltering night
we sped through farmland
on the way back
to the campsite.

107

in our deep-sea dives
the moon is what we miss
most of all,
no starfish
can compensate.

108

in a field of yellow daisies,
the white horse
is the moon
before the moon comes out.

109

the lemon forgotten
on the counter,
cast a hesitating
oval shadow
under the flickering
tube light.

110

every evening for years,
a deep-throated bell.
no clue who's being
summoned. i open
the door, just in case,
anticipate, hold my breath,
am greeted with silence.

111

she is nude,
skin white,
dances slowly,
warily like me.
we quicken
pace, burst
into flamenco,
curve, intersect,
unite.

112

the moon is a filter,
restoring me
to myself, cleansed.
also a recorder,
playing back my memories.

113

out the gate at Reno,
grabbing Route 580
to 431, you twist and turn
en route to Mt. Rose
as the moon peeks
in and out.

114

tiptoeing out of the bathtub,
sporting spiked heels
and wings, the moon tosses
a skimpy towel across
her shoulders, fashions
another into a turban
and rushes to the typewriter
to compose tall tales
no star would dare believe.

115

socks full of holes,
worn sandals,
frayed tunics,
buttons loose on shirts,
the universal genius
did the best he could
but got it all wrong.
darn that Ptolemy.

116

frankly, even
in her glory,
she was poor stuff
next to the moon.

117

standing up
to the stern half-moon,
and the straightedge
it brandishes,
a defiant world
disobeys each
and every decree
with relish.

118

skeletons
salute
the moon.

119

it's not the moon, brother,
you brought it upon yourself.
accuse, accuse, but place
blame where it's due.
for my part, i'm done
with stargazing. i've learned
my lesson; now learn yours.

120

when they said my wrestling
technique was beyond the pale
it was because I was helpless
in the face of my adversary
and found myself chiseled
to fit someone else's dream.

121

you shake the dice
and toss,

you shady sphere,
but don't play
by the rules,
advancing more
or less on whim.
stand back.
it's my turn now.

122

featured today at the Half Moon Club
is Rodrigo Montez and his band,
the Constellations, along with
that lovely trio of sisters,
the Bubbling Babes,
all for your earthly delight.

123

oysters open,
close, in rhythm
with waning,
waxing—wet
incarnation
of lunar spirit.

124

flooding through
an arching bow window,
the streams of light
congregating in a cantata
of praise for everything
they uncover are worthy
of the same.

125

startled deer
by the poplar grove.

blue moon betrays
sky primed for snow.
reflected people
in the glass lake—
an afterthought.

126

could no one
else have seen
what i saw
captured
in the petrified wood?

127

who can translate the wounds
the bandage covers into words
we won't have to grind
to comprehend? soon enough,
speechless, they will be felt.
there is always enough
pain to go around.

128

the inquisitive moon
is a silver question mark.

129

red-eyed
albino parakeet
in a black cage.

130

my daughter up
past her bedtime,

learning to tie
brand new shoelaces,
repeating it over
and again until
it becomes automatic.

131

always new riches
in the hollow between
your shoulder blades.
you flex and i land
far from where i started,
but who's complaining?

132

the jet takes off,
climbs ever higher.
the pilot says Louisville
but i have my own
itinerary.

133

the moon is hallucinatory
tonight. i fall asleep
on my recliner and summon
after-images of the streaming
tennis match.

134

sometimes it's weeks
i pay you no mind
and ask myself if
i've lost interest.
then, on a clear night
i find myself glued

to the window,
happily snubbing sleep.

135

he staked his heart
upon it and exulted
at prevailing
but in their eyes,
he lost the bet
that the moon would turn
transparent. he knew
it was no chimera
but alas, their truth
was not his.
no sense grousing.

136

flagpole points
straight up
and sure enough,
irrefutably,
to the target
you expected.

137

sometimes when i'm too proud
and vow to thrive without you,
i'm devastated by my own
folly before you
even have a chance to cackle
at my insecurity.

138

why is it during the day
you are not receptive
to unglazed porcelain

but when night arrives
you would trade in
the rainbow itself
for a white shard?

139

lightbulb reflected
in the windowpane.
for a moment you see it
as something else entirely.

140

it was no fable, the flowering
moon tree with nectar
that cures gravity.
you sip the lightness
with abandon.

141

enkindle the Japanese lantern
and you capture the moon.

142

bones of the carp
carry shiny secrets
to their final
resting place atop
the pond's muddy bottom.

143

how does a thistle
compare?
how many burrs
can you count
in the night
of a quarter moon?

144

what thug was it wrenched
the moon away from me
while my mind was elsewhere?
what a lowly lowlife theft,
jeopardizing my sanity,
upending my universe.
mark my words, i will not
let this pass.

145

for weeks, occupied with business
i considered essential, i shunned
the moon. with duties fulfilled
and anxious to rebuild relations,
i got my comeuppance when it turned
its back on me.

146

i grip the shallow, shimmering atmosphere
of the drawer's faceted glass pull,
and am transported to a better place.

147

the moon shines
through the eyes
of the black terrier.
my mood shifts
from despair
to amusement.

148

he is grateful but quivers
in the threadbare clothes
hand-me-downed
from the moon.

149

very much like eating
lemon yogurt
by half teaspoonfuls
in a dusky room.

150

a sparkling
crystal chandelier
crowns the dining room.
we pray for stability
while a cellist leans
into his ephemeral music,
all the more beautiful
for its transience.

151

the snowy owl turns
its head in a semi-circle,
following a white fragrance.

152

husks half-peeled, kernels gleaming,
breeze-blown tassels flapping,
two ears of corn listen intently
as they snuggle up to a red pitcher
by a half-open window commanding
a square view of an indigo sky
dominated by a yellowish orb
unmistakably speaking in tongues.

153

an ivory bird
named Luna
chirps at

the ringing of
the dinner bell
as if anticipating
a gift beyond
reckoning.

154

the moon is a radish
wavering on whether
to identify as red or white,
round or long, and whether
it should yield freely
in the harvest or hold its ground.

155

a dependable mattress
on a cold night. unexpectedly,
a blonde woman from long ago
turns up and grudgingly joins
me, climbing under the fluffy
blanket she never could abide.

156

an ebony wedding
band too large
for what it needs
to secure.

157

not worth our time
investing in another
useless argument
about the moon.
there are never winners
on nights like these.
no settling scores.

158

it comes in crystal clear,
overruling interference
from all quarters.
i get a kick showing
oblivious kids what's
what's in front of their eyes.

159

pewter urn in a white box,
gift wrapped in white
with a white bow—a present
for any occasion or none.

160

the roof puddles.
every raindrop
grins.

161

i had to blink.
in its place, overhead,
an enormous seashell,
crimson interior,
as patiently still
as what it replaced,
as unreal.

162

aluminum tacks
in corkboard,
private folded messages
telling me what i already know.

163

where have those keys gone?
i still feel traces in my fingers.
no worries, i tell myself.
the moon will open
doors i can't.

164

in Neptune Beach, Florida,
twenty sea turtle hatchlings
mistook streetlights
for the moonlit ocean,
wandered onto a road
and were crushed by cars.

165

snow concluded,
lone columnar elm,
winter silhouette,
shaving cream brush.

166

i thought i was done
with my obsession
but seeing your saffron
opulence in the rearview
mirror as traffic mounted,
it felt like we met
for the first time.

167

you suppose the sea
plays no role
but put your ear

to the giant conch shell
and you'll reconsider.

168

don't be surprised
if, in taking off
the lamp shade,
you find, instead
of a bulb, a presence
longer lived.

169

unwritten page blistered
with concealed moons
awaits the scribe's salve.

170

load the cannons.
there may be
no enemy yet
but be ready to fire.
you never know
where or when
on the horizon
one may materialize.

171

i went to sleep
with my wife
but woke up
with the moon.

172

tuberous crops,
potatoes, carrots,
low lying crops,

parsnip, radish—
hard tough
vegetables
where, incognito,
the moon hides.

173

awakened by a flash, i spy
two moons instead of one.
they tease me, make me question
my mental state. i yank them
from their domicile, shrink
them down to size, and seal
them in a canning jar. alarms
are set off, flares. i give up
searching for my camera, return
to a now empty jar, lid dislodged.
back in the wild blue yonder,
a singular moon grins for all its worth.

174

heartbeat of moon
keeps time
to universe still
in its infancy.

175

the moon is dispensed
like scotch tape
on a roll
and we are running
low.

176

unawares, i must have stumbled
into the moon after a woozy
drinking session for, reaching

home, i found myself powdered
with talcum and couldn't care less.

177

across a protracted winter,
a convoy of moons
march to ensure safe entry
for a long-craved spring.

178

alongside you on the magic
carpet where you sit spinning
a roulette wheel, the moon,
like a tame dove, waits,
preening itself, but ready
at a moment's notice,
once the Delrin ball drops
in the triple zero pocket,
to take flight and lead you
to your fated port of call.

179

i grow disoriented by concentrating on you
too intensely, can't stand straight, feel
off-kilter, cry out for support, am met
by nothing besides your blank stare
only upsetting me more.

180

periodically i get you
mixed up with the sun.
i fall when i should rise
and, bless your heart,
you forgive me all
i'm in your thrall.

181

after the shower, i discover
my terrycloth slippers
in orbit. soaking wet,
i speed after them.
the moon throws me
a towel and robe,
says there's no need
to hurry.

182

the moon is sharp
as dogtooth calcite.
not the first time
i have been bitten,
and i always walk
away changed.

183

misshapen waning
gibbous glows behind
yellow gingko leaves
drifting down
through dusky sky.

184

can you solve the riddle
of the moon on the griddle,
why its abundance
shrinks in circumference,
its middle frazzled
with hardly a sizzle?

185

espionage on the moon.
brown envelopes and cash

surreptitiously slink
from crater to crater.

186

under the pasty hide
of the moon—
a multi-colored secret
entrusted to its finder's
safekeeping.

187

don't contradict me
with facts if i want
to believe it's a place
where billions of Yoshino
cherry trees bloom forever.

188

we battle over its meaning
and our own, engage
in mock jousts to see
who can unmoon
the mysteries of earth.

189

up the endless ladder
to attain the goal,
up the infinite rope,
hand over hand.
none of it any good.
no better, the space
capsule's on-target
landing. reaching it
meaningfully
is a delusion.

190

you hear the words
i murmur, meant for no one,
your ear the harbor
of my deepest secrets,
and not mine alone.
how is it you are so
accommodating to so many?

191

i recognized the moon
hide-and-seeking
from under
the full black hair
of his otherwise
impervious beard.

192

on that ancient
Portuguese map
of the heavens,
why did they paint
you frowning?

193

don't let me detain you
from your rounds but
for a moment. just tell me,
are there any messages
for me from the other
side of my planet,
from anyone i miss
or that misses me?

194

open container of makeup powder
discovered behind bathroom sink
months later, layered
with hazy streaks of dust.

195

white tiger leaping
through flaming hoop
hasn't forgotten the jungle.
the jungle has forgotten him.

196

according to the Enigami tribe,
the full moon of June is the moon
of forgotten strawberries
because the crop has lessened
though not disappeared, yet
all their talk and sacrifices
are about berries still to be harvested.

197

when the only images that suffice
are musical, when a solo flute
is sufficient to taste the complexity
of the whole composition.

198

after-hours in the bakery
display case—cookie crumbs,
chocolate sprinkles, and half
a lemon meringue pie.

199

the Japanese speak not
of a man in the moon
but a rabbit pounding rice
into a paste to make mochi
cakes, sticky, stretchy,
soft and chewy. have one.

200

you walk empty avenues
with empty pockets
but, watched over,
don't feel bereft.

201

i close the cherry
wood desk drawer,
letting go the shiny
brass handle. it clinks
against the back plate,
glinting with a burst
of little crescents.

202

you fathom what i withhold.
bubbling up like an artesian well,
you carry me to the surface
to rethink my hesitancy.

203

i fret over you,
cousin introvert,
isolated
in a never ending

trajectory,
for your course
is not guaranteed.

204

lately, you break
through the clutter
of my mind
midday.
i take comfort
that, visible or not,
you are in
my crosshairs.
the shame of it
is i will lose you
when i'm gone.

205

i had scrutinized
your bare body
many times over
and never noticed
the resemblance
but last night
there was no mistaking
your manifold
and overlapping orbs,
front and back,
inside and out.

206

a child's game—lifting
him up so he can turn
the old-style parking meter
knob to flip the disks
back and forth.
red—time expired.
yellow—violation.

207

replacing the roll
of scotch tape
on the spool
tokened
a grander vision.

208

the abandoned ballroom
twirls still
with memories of dance.

209

slicing a cucumber,
i startle at the pale
greenness inside,
at the vulnerability
of its seeds.

210

what you wouldn't give
for another chance
at creation.

211

you must have been tailed
the length of the backstreet.
only realized it at the dead end,
when you turned and came
face to face with yourself.

212

the job was stuffing pillows.
the money wasn't much

but the down
was addictive.

213

late May—dogwood
comes into leaf
after flowers drop,
but here, weeks later,
unexpected and unapologetic,
an open, fragile, perfectly
white blossom.

214

flipping a blank spiral
notebook's pages
of faintly lined paper
can seduce you to scribble
or starkly remind you
of too many spells
of helplessness.

215

a cymbal struck
at birth, the shudder
of a clang
reverberating
ever after.

216

the Ashanti say Kwaku Anansi,
the spider, found a glowing globe
and could not choose which
of his six sons deserved it
for doing the most to rescue him
from the belly of the fish
and the jaws of the falcon,

so Kwame, the God of all things,
put it up in the sky, where it is
to this day.

217

my relief does not come.
the watch is prolonged.
these ramparts are impossible
to keep secure.
i move to the right,
my shadow to the left.

218

yellow moon? grey moon?
everybody, listen: "you waste
your energy second-guessing
the pre-ordained. gambling
on color is folly."

219

my breath,
a feather duster
sweeping away
inter-stellar dust
built up around you
over years of doubt.

220

the best summer nights
were when he'd hear
crickets chirp across
acres of countryside
and watch fireflies
construct a puzzle
of connect-the-dots
just for him.

221

you've become expert
at cascading the dark lager
down the tilting side
of the faceted glass stein
before setting it upright
and pouring more
to the tip of the rim
for a perfect head,
all prelude to taking
solid and well-paced
gulps to educate
your inquisitive innards
with the fizzy intelligence
of tiny sousing bubbles.

222

in the freezer aisle
huddled between pizza
and juice concentrates,
frosty and cramped,
you are mistaken for
lemon sherbet popping
out of its container.

223

in a grade school production,
she stood halfway up the ladder.
hanging from one shoulder,
a large cardboard crescent
covering most of her torso.
otherwise, she dressed in black,
played the backdrop
to two sweethearts
singing a duet.

224

put the tablet on your tongue.
flick it back in your mouth,
swallow, and stick
your empty tongue back out
for all to judge the proof.

225

the moon is not
a solitary mushroom.
it's the bullseye inside
a host of mushrooms,
a bevy of fungal cores,
yearning for revelation.

226

at the full-length haberdashery
mirror, the moon was fussing
with the angle of its derby
to make it complement the cut
of its smoking jacket.

227

the water tumbling over
Great Falls turned
into a chain of moons
swashing into the Potomac
and flowing downstream.

228

you made as if to kiss,
as if ready to be kissed.
it was the shape
of your lips, the shape
within, that stopped me
cold … momentarily.

229

i counted 45 theatrical masks
in the storefront's window.
white faces, hollowed eyes,
breathing hole noses,
and they were all looking
to me for answers.

230

cicadas, underground
seventeen years, ascend.
nymphs molt one last time
before taking flight,
a prequel to further drama,
all under the amused
and watchful eyes
of the moon.

231

take an impossibly thin
slice of onion.
slice it a thousand times
finer. position one piece
against the sky
to unearth an optics
worth crying over.

232

a tonic before bed—
a sparkling beverage
to contradict
the lunacy
of the day
and make all
well again.

233

Tsukimi
is what the Japanese
call moon gazing
at the pristine Harvest
Moon in the clear sky
of September. in Osawa
Pond, we sip tea
in dragon boats.
one moon above us,
one below—the same,
different.

234

in daylight hours
before chu-shu no meigetsu,
Japanese Harvest Moon,
you already sense its presence—
in the quivering maple leaves
and the coolness of her cheeks.
you live it thoroughly,
insight trumping sight.

235

the finality of your slamming
the door shut behind you
this time, unlike all the rest,
cannot be undone, no matter
how many times
you prod it open again.

236

a massive circular planter
of impatiens overflowing.
water from a sprinkler
not well positioned

soaks into the concrete
column supporting its base.

237

peeling an apple. setting it
on the glass plate,
committedly monitoring
the flesh as it darkens
to brown.

238

a cylindrical glass
paperweight of marbles
in a viscous liquid.
turn it upside down.
they descend lazily.
reverse position.
back they fall
not quite as slowly.
it takes so little
to entrance you.

239

white socks—mine,
my son's, my father's.
all the white socks
in the world—linkages,
irrefutable or tenuous,
are not to be ignored.

240

the sails billow.
the moon drops anchor.
we board and leave
cares behind.
we embark
to pick up more.

241

inside the jack-o-lantern,
the moon,
inside the moon,
the jack-o-lantern.

242

steel wheels of the train,
trace points on the tracks,
accelerate, briskly etch
unforgettable lines
of voyages past
and present
onto the rails.

243

non-conforming pillow
refuses to set a proper well
for your exhausted head,
which swells from the lumpy
pressure, and rebuffs
your too crowded brain's
endless quest for respite.

244

on any one of a number of days
he might easily have drifted off
to eternity but willed himself
to hold out until the next full moon
when, by custom, he had the nurse
roll his feeble wheelchaired body
to the roof deck where, in mind
of a better place, he expired,
happy and without regrets.

245

sometimes the moon
gives me a migraine,
it pains me to concede,
and makes me reconsider
what i want of it. i grow
weary of its tranquility.
i want it to flare up
like the sun.

246

my insides disclose
fractures glowing
on an X-ray.
how is it i never
felt a thing?

247

it has been a long while,
and not to my credit,
since i gave up
venerating this
or any nightly guest.
if only i could snap
out of my irreverence,
i swear i would never
let myself go
lax again.

248

shaking the clear
acrylic salt tumbler,
she pours grains
of the moon,
onto a baked potato.

249

on the barren landscape,
stubby bases of white
marble columns,
remnants of a temple.
yes, i remember now,
how we toiled
in the construction,
and to think it's come to this.

250

calla lilies in a vase
on the wooden porch
railing at night.
the first guests
are making their entrance.

251

strawberries and cream.
where does one end
and the other begin?

252

mining for soft coal
in hostile tunnels, you ignore
your comrades' early warnings.
they are powerless to answer
your too late calls.

253

in the hole chewed
by an anonymous insect,
the moon becomes one
with a milky rose petal.

254

nobody but my son claimed
to catch sight of you
and he wasn't mistaken
for he wanted to see you
more than anyone
and had patience to spare.

255

white duck
uncoupled from clan,
paddling bottomless
algal waters.

256

carved of walrus tusk,
suspended in the sky
like the eye of a walrus,
all-seeing, and i row
the walrus sea
with a brawny need.

257

what is it with this
obsession of yours—
boiled eggs piled high
in a cone? forgive me
while i set them tumbling.

258

the moon granted me more
than i could ever use
but i was never satisfied.
how selflessly it gave

while i lied to its face
about my need. i stood
my ground, but shame
set my legs to trembling.

259

objective sighted.
a clear shot. ignition.
sever umbilicals.
a measured burst.
launch. jackpot!
as good as there.

260

moonstone walls
support the vault of heaven.
my fault is that i want
the roof to shatter over me
for an unfettered view,
yet be immune to injury
from falling shards
or blinding light.

261

the moon has taken enough
turns around the block
to subscribe to the big bang
but doesn't have a clue
how it will end.

262

catching the carousel's brass
rings is no challenge but
after a few revolutions
they turn to moons. you close
and open your eyes, blink

and blink, but it's a fact,
leaving you stretching
to no avail, reaching for
but never reaching.

263

on this oppressive night
the moon stays cool
while i sweat drops
of envy.

264

the moon at my wedding,
shoving its way in between
the groomsmen and bridesmaids,
wielding a knife to cut the cake.
no, that's too ludicrous a fiction.
my bride—she's the moon
…or is it me?

265

the moon shrinks down
to one dimension
and then the point is gone.
it had been everything
but now is lost like me.
rebirth, an eternity away,
comes in a flash.

266

hurled my way, i'm struck
out by the moon, consistently
in the zone, leaving me
dazed and dazzled
by heavenly arcs.
i can hardly imagine

swinging, and stand
like a statue, moonstruck.

267

too loaded
on cosmic space,
you become boastful,
unlike yourself,
a delinquent unwilling
to learn, a gangster
too sure of himself.

268

nobody is surprised
anymore when you step
out of orbit, out of line,
indifferent at losing
your bearings.
you've been there
and they've seen it
all before. there will be
no fallout. you'll still be
worshipped.

269

stacks of scholarly moons,
finger-food hors d'oeuvres
on platters carefully balanced
by waiters at the opening
of the astrophysical conference.
who can help but surrender
to such miniature nibbles?

270

at the reception,
one hundred brews

of the moon—
an array of frosty
draughts to suit
any palate,
more phases
than you can imagine,
for your imbibing
pleasure.

271

in a quandary
about a place
to stay? choose
the Moonbeam Motel.
take Highway 99
to where it peaks.
park the car
and keep going.
it's worth the climb!

272

tumbling down
mountain streams,
whispering to peacocks,
comporting himself with flair,
giving sage counsel, looking
for all the world
like a most foreign ambassador
presenting his eminence,
himself, to the visionaries
among us who can recognize
him without explanation.

273

could it be the lightning
bugs have come down to tell us

what we wouldn't know
unless we looked up?

274

a diver directing
a light beam
at the coral reef.
crevices scoop
up every wavelength.

275

the moon
is a brightly lit underpass
going from man's side
to God's. we traverse,
without signposts,
the unflickering white
eternal from memory.

276

granted, it sheds
some paltry light,
tugs at us
with piddling gravity,
and is a backdrop
for fanciful tales
but it moves us most
as a stand-in
for that unattainable
other—love.

277

in the path of sunlight,
you are bleached
with sorrowful black
shadows, but after hours,

you take heart and ripen
to spectral white
under the therapeutic
gaze of the moon.

278

the moon multiplies.
now two, now four
pop up from the toaster,
crisp and ready for a spread
of butter and jam. breakfast
is served. don't be late.

279

wearing a glow-in-the dark
headband and skillfully
maneuvering a unicycle,
she holds a book on asteroids
up to her face, pretending
to read, but two small holes
drilled through the pages
allow her to see exactly
where she's going.

280

you learned the language easily
enough but the moon grows
impatient with your thick accent
and how often you lapse
into your native tongue. maybe
for some small change, you can
hire those lumpy satellites of Mars,
Phobos or Deimos, to interpret.

281

inexplicable,
such a loss.

down on his knees,
in front of the newborn
wrapped in white,
he lowers his head,
cries for the infant
that no longer can.

282

the moon is shaped
like a coconut. its flesh,
moist coconut fruit.
it tastes of coconut milk,
and hairy coconut skin
is what mine has become
as i stand in solidarity.

283

clusters of berries,
hugging each other,
sweet talking each other,
bursting and falling
with blessings of the bush.

284

scattered evidence, indistinct,
lightly traced, fading, in stems
of night-blooming cereus
in the morning, before sun
takes charge, obliterating vestiges
with uncompromising brightness.

285

"lift me up," the child pleads,
"i still can't. higher, higher."
"yes, now i can," he exults,
"i'm touching it now."

286

a silly moon, preposterous,
sporting a moustache,
a wriggling moustache,
rubber nose, and Chaplin
derby, with claptrap notions
of planetary motions,
mischievously spraying
the sky with moonlit ditties
through a water hose,
a clownish pantomime,
the perfect antidote
to solemn, earthly notes.

287

gushing rain
carrying cryptic messages
from afar, overflows the bucket
and is strained through
ever finer screens to reach
the tonic's finest concentrate.

288

grandma's china set
trotted out for his party.
each child's dessert plate
rimmed with gilded
indentations, shallowly
scalloped, for serving
up wedges of frosted vanilla
buttercream cake, and seconds.

289

we succeeded in carving it
down to a cube, much easier
to handle and store, less
unwieldy. we couldn't have it

spinning away forever—
too frivolous. the excess went
to fabricate smaller cubes—
spares for other planets
should the need arise.

290

perhaps the ball
the elephant balances
on his trunk. perhaps
the white Muslim kufi
cap adorned with elephants
on the head of its rider.

291

keeps itself tucked
out of sight 'til ready
to bloom and loom,
impactful counterpoint
to flashy comets et al
clamoring for attention.

292

on heaven's slate,
a moon dissolves.
its fading reign
an illusion, though,
for it returns to dominate
the play long after
you have quit the scene.

293

popcorn moon bobs up
one night to intercept
a stretch of murky boredom.
it takes a maize agronomist

to identify the species.
luckily, we are all experts.

294

scant breaths away
from dozing, i'm knocked
off my feet by a bulldozer
moon daring me to take
charge of my life. i glare
it into a cower, satisfying
us both.

295

like a bell rung at random,
not to mark a beginning
or end, or signify much
of anything other
than a celebration
of continuity.

296

for you alone, i dropped
a diamond bracelet in a well.
dip deep to unpuzzle
its echo, and you'll hear me
loud and clear from on high.

297

in the market, examining
half melons, orange fleshed.
not that one is any better
than the rest but that being
human makes you think it so.

298

hedgehog moon slinking
between clouds, why
do you ball yourself up?
come now, unravel.
there are no predators
up where you are.

299

off the golf course,
off the charts,
your greatest drive,
its apogee, inevitable.

300

knock knock on the moon's door,
knock knock. i insist, "let me in,"
and knock again 'til the annoyed
footman peeks out the peephole.
"what ho, what racket?"
"i'm wanting in, you fool."
"you are in already, sir."
"a technicality," i countered,
"let me in anyway."

301

falling for the moon,
in over my head. not expecting
anyone to understand, i turn
spongy, pliant, am entangled
in its roots and swept up
repeatedly by its undercurrent
with no regrets.

302

weeks on end, i anticipated
a joyful alert but was met,
in the end, by absence and hurt.

303

you kiss the void.
i know it's meant
for me. what else,
out of the blue,
would honor me
with such benefit
of doubt?

304

what if we squeezed the big ball
down to a pea and buried it inside
the sleeping farmer's mattress?
what crops, what vines! wake up,
Farmer Brown, surprise!

305

hail, moon, transmuting
and enduring through the years,
new to old to new. diapers
transmogrify to ancient
tattered smocks and back,
sleight of hand couture.

306

you're a fraud
to pass yourself off
as a herald of romance.
i'm sick of your illusions.
leave me to the little

dignity i have left.
no, i take it back.
give me another day
to feed on false hopes.
who knows?

307

how lucky my noticing,
dear moon, your skating
on ice in a figure eight,
imitating infinity, frozen,
and infinitely recurring.
watching, i find my bearings.
why don't we join forces?
give me a minute to lace up.
we'll make an enviable twosome.

308

the moon
is a miracle
quite like everything
the moon is not.

309

moon's modesty
enlivens. what joy
to wake early
with the birds
and bid you
good day
before bully sun
throws its weight around.

310

airplane exhaust trail draws
a faint question mark

around the object
of your wonder.
it would be a greater wonder
if an answer materialized,
ever.

311

a roll of the dice,
so like the fall
of duck pins
in a strike.
it's all a gamble.

312

i press my palm
against my forehead
but am no wiser.
i press harder still
and am not enlightened.
i release, making everything
worse. unlike my ever
optimistic friend,
i cannot start over.

313

under the spotlight,
straining to saw
through cello strings
with the bow,
his bald head frowns.
someone in the front row
throws him a pair of scissors.
he smiles from ear to ear.

314

against the inside
of the outhouse back wall,

opposite the crescent moon
carved door, the sun slaps
a shadow twin.

315
the way he celebrated
winning a race
was to swing his right
running shoe over
his head and send it
flying into the trajectory
of victory.

316

evenly matched, we draw
battle lines. caution goes
to the wind and we submit
to providence provided
our opponent is trounced.

317

tagua nut, ivory textured
flesh, turned like wood
into a miniature container
to hold nothing per se
but, rather, reveal
the rich kernel within.

318

what unseen hands have molded
our aspirations into that giant
rotating ball fit to occupy
a lifetime's contemplation?

319

eyes of sightless fish
retrieved from ocean bottom

handed out to blind science
lab students to dissect
and investigate with senses
at hand while microscopes
gather dust in a corner.

320

have you ever smelled
the moon, that white
delicacy that fills
chocolate space?
have you ever trusted
anything so distant
and reliably inconstant?

321

on a treadmill, not advancing,
not arriving. going but never
gone, carrying on, being carried
far off and high, at least in spirit,
forever and never, for once.

322

untold pages to fill.
how long will they stay
empty? how many
blank books waiting
for the right words?

323

watch the tablet
fizz blue in the water.
tiny battalions of bubbles
scaling heights, bursting
under my nose, tickling,
daring me to chuckle.

324

i want to go down
to underground caverns
and find my way
to the sky. i want
to parachute down
to the fiery core and soft
land in a cool, dark place.

325

sitting barefoot on the grass
alongside the river, face skyward
and a cotton ball in her hand.
one moment her smile eclipses
her eyes and the next, its her eyes
eclipsing her smile. bending over,
she finishes wiping the red
from her toes. now unadorned,
ten streaks of light sparkle,
eclipsing the night.

326

no, i haven't the faintest
what's in your fist. slyly,
you intimate it could be
anything, and who am i
to doubt? truly, anything,
you repeat, to drive
the point home, even
more than fits. i press
your fingers back in
as you begin to loosen
them, and beg for a few
more moments of suspense.

327

out of sight, the moon,
preoccupied with its own
obligations, discloses more
to me than in outward
declarations when it's front
and center.

328

if you set the shallow,
empty offering bowl
on the windless rocky
ledge, to rest undisturbed,
how many millennia
would it take for cosmic dust
to pile up to its rim?

329

the gleaming bulb
of wavering
decisions can be right
at any given moment
but is predisposed
to shift at a moment's notice.

330

i am spellbound
by celestial mooing.
what can i offer you
to find me a spot
of pasture to join
in your bovine
contentedness?

331

behind your arbitrary glow,
myriad intentions escape,
divulging what's missing
in the defused poker
face you show the world.

332

like the toreador with his cloak,
passing it over the bull,
the clouds do their toying
but spare us in not coming in
for the kill.

333

manifold hands
open, a handful
extend, a scant
few touch
and one, ideal
in conformation,
cups in mine.

334

i gargled so long,
i lost control
and swallowed
the spherical
capsule whole.

335

after harried commute, quick
groceries, serving dinner,
cleaning up, helping kids

with homework, TVing
and husband-comforting,
when all quiets down,
off i blast.

336

a convoy of ants carrying
luminous tribute
on their backs, across
the backyard and up
to the shed's slanted roof,
laying it down in a circle,
an end-of-month ceremony
scrupulously observed.

337

when gales howl,
the scarecrow moon
hops a ride, sprinkles
its straw filling
on windswept trails
until it expires
from a surfeit
of emptiness.

338

first off, i write
the recipient's address
on the envelope, then
my own, and affix a stamp.
i slide it to a corner
of the orderly desk,
hold my pen over
a glaringly vacant
sheet of paper, stare
and stare but can't
bear to start.

339

diving into the flame,
racing through layer
upon layer of singeing
heat quickly enough
to escape the worst,
you emerge
in a frosty oasis
with no desire
to thaw
for a long, long while.

340

the moon was arraigned
before the fifth circuit court
but judged incompetent
to stand trial
and it suited the moon
just fine for it had grown
wobbly and insecure
and was sure
to perjure itself.

341

stuck on the moon again,
that infernal kite.
i've learned my lesson,
though, and won't bother
trying to reel it in.
one bounding jump
will get me there.

342

to see it properly from inside
inside the house, i had to turn
off the pervasive ceiling lights,

intense floor lamps, mood-
setting table lamps, and dim
night lights, and strip off
my wristwatch with its photo-
luminescent face, all intrusions
that threaten to ambush
a focusing mind.

343

the turnstile, circling
horizontally, leads
to a vertical revolving
door, imprinting you
with a mental afterimage
of cylinders run amuck
on the verge of expanding
into a myriad of dimensions.

344

the ragged moon,
in bad shape tonight,
sizes me up for a handout
but is too down and out
to fathom we are brethren
in misfortune.

345

i run to the left and come
smack up against the moon.
i run to the right—again
the moon. i stay put, shut
my eyes—no respite. i pray
for a different outcome
and hear it whispering
for the same.

346

pink liquid soap
in a plump bottle.
many pumps,
bottle after bottle,
many dollops,
much washing,
rinsing, drying.
clean living
takes work.

347

i stole slowly
from the bedroom
to keep you from guessing
too soon by the finality
of my steps on the creaky floor
that i was leaving for good
but you knew full well
what to expect long before
it ever entered
my muddled mind.

348

my son proposed we play
catch with an invisible energy ball.
he is five and an old hand
at make-believe. how could i
deny him such a game?
so, we alternately thrust out
and cupped our empty hands.
i was embarrassed by the teenagers
keeping an eye on us until one
quite seriously shouted,
"throw it here, pop."

349

waist-deep in moonlight, i want
to sink further so i can rise
higher, to submerge myself
in its aura and emerge soaking
wet as it drips from me
and i inhale without consequence
its tenuous atmosphere.

350

i am shadowed by a megalith
broken away from mother moon.
it thinks i need a personal body-
guard and won't let up.
i am not grateful. go away,
overanxious boulder. go back
to mamma, who is ample enough
to comfort the lot of us on her own.

351

i am lulled by the cadence
of the grandfather clock,
hands sweeping across
its Chinese numeraled face,
and cherish swinging
on the pendulum
of indecipherable time.

352

impatiently, interminably
i press the green button
for the up elevator.
isn't anyone listening?
or do they think me,
stalled, stranded
at the lowest level

with no other means
of escape, an unworthy
petitioner. i keep pressing,
hoping against hope.

353

after the opera,
from the orchestra pit,
a tuba's leftover echo—
foghorn in the night.

354

the sun's pull vies with mine.
it outdoes me in mass, energy
and downright dazzle but i
overcome with nearness
and consideration. its tug
is coercive, mine, intimate
and persuasive.

355

wood blind slats slice
and layer our guest. twist
wand counterclockwise—
all is cloaked. clockwise,
and she's restored.

356

the moon in the storm
highlights the furious
mood of the storm
like your own
stormy mood
at the relentless
storming moon.

357

bus shelter. bright night.
you open bifocal eyeglass case,
see double, and are too hypnotized
to remove the pair to read
the schedule. besides, the bus
is here. you jump on board.
bi-fold doors close behind you.

358

anchoring the lawn, a venerable
cornus florida, white flowering
dogwood, petals at maximum
spring spread, sure to brown
any day now, and be succeeded
by glossy green summer leaves,
reddening and joining forces
with scarlet berries as the year
progresses, with only a few
hanging on as the tree airs out
for its winter interlude.

359

Joshua Slocum—the first man
to sail alone around the world
in his boat, "Spray," completed
his journey on July 3, 1898,
returning to Fairhaven, Mass.
on the Acushet River, three
years later. a routine pastime of his
was talking to the man in the moon.

360

i was practicing the dance steps
in time to the wildly spinning

gyrations of my partner but the tempo
of the moon's measured orbit interfered,
and we crisscrossed and stumbled
too much for our own good.

361

it's contracted and fallen,
landed in the white wine
glass. see it swirl
like a shining marble,
decelerate, and metamorphose
into a glow-worm searching
the bowl's interior for a mate.

362

i did not mean to skewer you
with my blade, only to prick
the skin of your chest, but you
lunged at me more forcefully
than i expected. i could see
you understood and forgave me
before you fell, face up,
never to rise. my everlasting thanks.

363

you ask why i keep dredging
this ancient river at night.
i say it's because it scares me
imagining what it hides.

364

i knew when you pulled
up your sleeve to show me
the dial of your watch
you did not mean

to give me a lesson
in time, nothing
so sinister.

365

arriving above tree line,
a big ache leaves my heart
and i'm lightened in more ways
than one by the leafless,
piercingly neutral sky.

366

the moon is a springboard
to space beyond the moon,
to my innermost
inverse cosmos.

367

he dynamited the mill
for no other reason
than to see giant puffs
of flour rise
over the waterfront
and whiten the yachts.

368

the moon, pockmarked,
stubbly chin, donning
a dirty baseball cap,
down on its luck.
i flip a silver dollar high
up in the air. a "thanks,
buddy" wink tells me
it reaches its mark.

369

a lozenge, my medicine,
dissolving in my mouth,
circulating inside me,
mending my system,
doing its work so i can
do mine.

370

impulsive Tsukuyomi, Japanese god
of the moon, repulsed by the cooking
techniques of the goddess of food,
Uke Mochi, at a banquet, slew her
on the spot, prompting his sister, wife,
and goddess of the sun, Amaterasu,
to flee from his cruelty and Tsukuyomi
to pursue her across the heavens
for all eternity. thus, night and day
were forever separated.

371

an iridescent fountain sprays
clouds of foam under the jowls
of cherubs, giddily delighted
by the attention.

372

A Collection of Craters:

    Rabbi Levi, Racal, Racine
    Raspletin, Razumov, Respighi

A Sampling of Seas:

    Mare Angurs—Serpent Sea

Mare Crisium—Sea of Crises
Mare Fecunditatis—Sea of Fecundity
Mare Marginis—Sea of the Edge
Mare Serenitatis—Sea of Serenity
Mare Tranquillitatis—Sea of Tranquility

A Miscellany of Mountains:

Agnes, Blanc, Hadley,
Herodotus, Maraldi, Vitruvius

373

sometimes it's unmistakable, smacks
you in the face. other times obscure,
requiring excavation. every now
and then so patently absent
that you know you're being fooled
and it must, just must, be there.

374

what is left for me say to you, old moon,
my second self? the hours i've spent
in your study are a pittance next to those
you focused on me. you know
my goings to and fro, and on, and all
my silent needs better than i. direct
your shaft my way just now when i am
out of sorts and surely i'll come to
terms with myself and, world-wide,
spread word of your good deeds.

375

after a long convalescence
of pleasure blended with pain,
i reluctantly recuperated
from the sharply piercing
axis of the moon.

376

one after one, he severed
the lotus pods from their stems
and set them in the water
to fashion a twin galaxy adrift
and expanding downstream.

377

moon fleetingly disclosed
behind thick dividing clouds,
subject to the whims
of the wet night
struggling to forget.
i grieve in tandem,
shedding useless tears
for memories too stubborn
to budge.

378

rising moon ahead,
setting sun, behind.
my shell-shocked brain
fails to cope, turning,
spinning, juggling,
fatigued enough
to opt for anything—
to no avail.

379

i clutch opposite edges
of the chair's seat
to catch hold of my nerves
and keep myself
from springing across
distances too vast
to fathom.

380

baby cries at midnight.
you robe, hurry.
rocking her in your arms
doesn't do the trick
so, you carry her
to the porch swing.
at last, she is calmed
by the comforting sway,
you take it, not noticing
what else transfixes her.

381

holding up the convenience store,
his first time, wasn't worth it,
he concludes, counting the money
where he parked several blocks away.
a decent take but no joy in it.
he reclines, wondering
what's worth anything.

382

the moon, a balloon,
bursting, too soon,
a ruin.

383

on the abandoned wharf,
while the city snores, i practice
dueling with a razor-edged sword,
glittering sides. i thrust, lunge
at the firmament and shred
emptiness into diaphanous ribbons
which form themselves back
into an impervious shield.

384

cracked ice on the sidewalk.
i am shattered
by your broken promises.

385

big white angular
rocks pockmarking
Japanese blood grass
on the slope of a hill.
a tremor. the one topmost
rolls down, bumps another,
and then a cascade.
i enter and exit
multiple dreams.

386

angling the back of her hands
up and tilting her neck
parallel to get a good view
of her fingernails, primed
for a layer of red polish.
tides rise, blood rushes
to her head.

387

who knows in how many
other caves in the Pyrenees
are hidden stones like these,
with 29 nearly faded dots
of paint in ocher, red, or brown,
followed by a tiny diagonal
scratch, and what, for certain,
they may signify.

388

wildly zooming down highway 7,
wind whisking my hair, fluttering
my clothes, i seatbelt myself
onto the moon, and obsessively
take out the artificial road lights
with slingshot and lead pellets.

389

like latching
onto a hook,
i hang
from its edge
with a long
unflinching
look.

390

first quarter sickle.
there is threshing
afoot. let me join.
i can lend a hand.

391

a night sun of sorts,
you are brightness
diminished at daybreak
here but still in your prime
a few degrees distant.
someone is always watching.
for you, privacy was not
in the stars but you've grown
accustomed to adulation.

392

can one insert a patch
of light into the empty
speculation adjoining
concavity to overcome
natural proclivities? "no
indeed," saith the sage,
"even stray thoughts
of thwarting destiny
will backfire."

393

a forceful squeeze of the atomizer
and it exhales innumerable aerosols,
each a perfectly formed moon
in miniature, glowing
with the accrued light of creation.

394

diminished by half
of what you'd been,
you know better
than to gripe because
you're also half
of what you'll become.
no infirmity, this.
you are confident
and grin in full.

395

don't be self-conscious about size,
little buddy. you and i know
that in the scheme of things,
we're both specks. let's focus
on brightening things up

for those other miniscule creatures
like ourselves absentmindedly
scampering about.

396

the moon—a tomb
of relics, dead
sanctuary, reservoir
of longing, and jumping
off point for life
as we know it
not.

397

you are a vial of fulfillment.
what more could we ask
than to also be refilled
before we are depleted,
to be renewed in advance
no less than you?

398

pull-offs are many
along the thruway
to the terminus
but why dally
when it's easily
within reach?
don't rest until you've left
the rest behind.

399

i step out of the planetarium.
country autumn night.
birds, insects, sky, whatever

i need to hear and see
is here. i don't begrudge
the telescope but am better
off foregoing intermediaries.

400

perfect, tearless
onion of fluorescence,
this science museum
model on my bedstand.
it freshens the palate,
makes me long for salad.

401

many a time together, we ogled
our planetary mate, me flat
on the grass, hands clasped
behind my neck, stationary,
you with your legs drawn up
to your belly, arms enfolding
them, rocking back and forth.
we rarely spoke about anything
of consequence. now, watching
all alone, i visualize the ball
you rolled yourself into
that i never could untangle.

402

will it crack like an egg
if it falls, Mommy, will it?
like Humpty Dumpty?
when does it move, Mommy?
it's always someplace else
but i never see it move.
it always goes away.
will it always come back?

403

carrying dull gray pewter pots
filled to the brim with moon-
berries, we frolic in the woods,
tossing them to birds already
drunk but in no condition
to abstain. we overeat the fruit
ourselves, deplete the containers,
and turn them into drums
we beat with fallen twigs.
inverted, they convert
to helmets for our promenade.
the birds trail us in tipsy flight.

404

at the western end of the Avenue
of the Dead, dating to Teotihuacan,
sits the Pyramid of the Moon, a
site for ritual sacrifices and burials,
second in size to the nearby Pyramid
of the Sun, playing second fiddle
as always.

405

i wrestled with you
playfully in a dream.

you grew tentacles
and wrapped me tightly.

in love, we rolled up
and down hills we loved,

indistinguishable
from each other.

the complicit sky
sanctioned us with a wink.

406

generic hotel, generic city.
11th floor, 11th hour.
on the balcony, your tense
eyes seize the exit ramp
of the theatre's garage
across the street. wild
panther eyes of liberated cars
ready to rock, punch holes
in the fog. each radiant circle
beckons you to cling.

407

purple moon in November.
on these sullen nights of neglect,
you are too distracted to recognize
what the sky offers. obscuring
your mistakes, the violet tinged
halo is camouflage and target both.

408

the taut smoothness
of your elbow
when you bend
your arm to brush
a stray lock of hair
from your forehead.

409

my table set for the moon,
i serve wine. it chooses red
and i, white. i pour. we toast.

the moon raises its glass
to the limitless canopy.
with mine, i salute the moon.

410

i am atop a ridge.
the moon is no closer.
i stand on a mountain peak.
the moon as far away
as ever. in an airplane—
status quo. i nod off.
the moon brushes
against my cheeks.

411

triangles of moonlight
clatter down the curtain
folds onto the bed
and your naked arm
sticks out of the blanket
as if aiming at a dream
you're in the middle of.

412

i bowl a strike,
pins clattering—moon.
my parrot grooms
my graying beard—moon.
the bottom of the soup bowl
about to be filled—moon.
q-tipping my ear—moon.
i hesitate to admit it
but sometimes i outright
tire, totally, of moon.

413

when i spin
marbles,
they accumulate
as much color
as they lose,
become a blur
as if i myself
am spinning.

414

dipping your ladle
into the never-ending
tureen of memory
you scoop out
barrelsful of soup,
the level not shrinking
a jot.

415

the unenlightened know no better
than to dismiss the squawking
cockatoo as relentlessly noisy
for no cause when it is lucidly
calling attention to a common-
place lofty miracle.

416

wielding a sharp saber, advancing
on the moon and, with sweeping
slashes, undressing it, layer
by blessed layer until you reach
an inner sanctum leading to your own.

417

a tablespoon of moon
before bedtime.
unparalleled therapy
for the insomniac.

418

from behind the barred
window of my cell,
i pray for a slice
of your compassion
to rescue me
from this captivity.

419

miserable, i turn
the corner and see you
above the hill or
do you see me first?
no matter. at last, a link
that doesn't disappoint.

420

i tell myself
        you can lighten
        the load of night
        but know too well
        you can't.
i tell myself
        you can spark
        a dormant love
        but don't fool myself
        into believing it
i tell myself
        you are immaterial,

inconsequential,
have no bearing
on the road i traverse.
i only wish.

421

remnants on the ground,
lost, found, recurring
residuals abandoned,
reclaimed, cyclical.
pieces reassemble
before they vanish,
disintegrate as they are
discovered.

422

driven loony by this fixation
on the moon, i've no one
but myself to blame.
to be startled out of mind-
less vacancy was promising,
alerting me to be alert,
riling me, carrying me, up.
but i wandered too close
to the edge and dropped free-
fall, depleted, back to earth,
ever to regret what i surrendered.

423

the moon is a symbol
standing in for longing
and regret, all i'd wanted
to say, all i'd hoped to hear,
the clash of a cymbal calling
me back from my thoughtless
wandering. straighten up,
man, look alive!

424

do not succumb, fidgety
moon, to your situation
or give in to your worst
fears of being rent asunder.
take heart, and a breath.
gather strength from our pull.
we are here for you.

425

like a flag in outer space
raised nightly by our creator
and waving for all who see
and all who are blind. let us
stand and give an ovation
of patriotic acclaim.

426

a stray prospect of success,
expanding just enough
to forestall the dismal
foreboding of heartbreak.

427

the teacher takes his place
front and center. don't be
stuck-up. take yours
as a supplicant, one of many.
there's much to learn, first
off that being overshadowed
is no disgrace.

428

the dial-tone
when you hang

up on me—
musical,
reverberating,
conclusive.

429

go ahead—
sprinkle salt
on the egg
white.
pierce
the yolk.
wait
for inspiration.

430

i wonder if,
before time
runs out,
you will rescue me
and if i am
worth saving.

431

the moon, a tepid bowl
of goat milk swirling
in a heaven circulating
around a nucleus
impossible to isolate.

432

soldiers fed up with marching
set down their shields, spears,
fortitude, let down their guard,
sleep long past reveille, scruples
and bugles notwithstanding.

433

alright then, i'll take your bait
and cast caution to the wind.
a few swigs of that moonshine
before i sign off and slip out
of the light can't hurt. 150 proof,
you say? skoal! to my health!

434

i can better sense
through sheets
of driving rain
what i am meant
to behold and what
to disregard.

435

let me pay court to you,
Selene. don't be transfixed
by that ever youthful, ever
slumbering immortal mortal,
Endymion. you'll need no tricks
from Zeus to gain my eternal
devotion. my heart is already
yours. i'll worship at your altar,
no strings attached.

436

open wide but not your mouth.
take the cure optically.
the remedy, ironically,
will linger longer, stronger.

437

all told, i do well enough
to decode your manifold

shapes. tonight, though,
too scattered to interpret
your cryptic ovalness,
i prefer being kept
in the dark, and vow
not to whine.

438

like temple gongs, your music
gathers the faithful
and reminds me
of neglected obligations.

439

half under the shed
propped up on posts,
a little puddle,
the final trace
of last week's downpour,
insistently refuting
mindlessness.

440

inside-out softness,
the moon is a resting
place, a feather bed,
the refuge of last resort.

441

a scofflaw marshmallow
evades the skewer
of roasting, escapes
the cookout entirely,
rolls downhill, zigzagging
through neighborhoods,
wily fellow, incognito,
unreachable.

442

overlapping, amorphous patches
of brown and white
on the dog's flank echo
the layered racket of her bark,
befuddling my senses.

443

hidden between
the elephant's toes,
treasures yet to be
revealed, restored,
reconstituted, certain
to trigger cravings
that cannot be governed.

444

like a tablet that cushions
the banging in your head
the moment it dissolves—
analgesia in orbit.

445

for the Mohawk people,
it goes by the name
tsothohrha or cold moon
when full in December,
bordering on the winter
solstice. feel the chill.

446

how i miss the jokes
you told in the old days
when we downed beer
after beer in the wee hours.

how carefree you were then
before you swore off
drink and familiarity.

447

she promises
and i believe.
she inundates my eyes
with so much light
that i can't see.
she promises
and she deceives.

448

nobody believes the moon
is sane anymore, least of
all the moon. it rambles
on in defense of luminescence
as if this were an alibi.

449

over continents, oceans,
and atmosphere, you sweep
over all in your own good
time, for our own good,
or so you would have us
believe as you overwhelm
pretenses and uncertainties.

450

a wandering sail
transports us
to ports of call
we don't anticipate
and can't recognize
until an interstellar

wind nudges us along
to the boundary
of discovery.

451

atop camels' backs,
saddlebags filled with
dusty tales, dead weight
unintelligible in the heat.
pilgrims sweating
under fiery skies, straggle
on with them until night.
making camp, they set down
blankets, rouse themselves
and hearken to stories,
triggering epiphanies
like firework blasts.

452

a resurrected wooly mammoth
nudges up against you
affectionately, the thumping
heart inside its shaggy hulk
in accord with your aspirations.
you follow its upward curving
tusks to far beyond where they end.

453

you wash me clean
with soapy, sudsy intent,
drain away the errors
of creation, restore me
to what i can at least pretend
was a pristine beginning.
the layers of film that masked
me are stripped away.

what a relief not to be
weighed down with obscurity,
to anticipate a new future,
bright and unencumbered.

454

far removed, i pine
as you shrink, grow
despondent as you ebb.
losing sight completely,
i lose faith, am a wreck,
even though i know
better. my knees buckle
and i quake, waiting
for you to reemerge.

455

i don't remember seeing
this hue, this intensity
before, not in marigolds,
butter, bananas, egg yolks,
or the sun (and that's saying
something) or been so startled
and confused by yellow.

456

the dragon is melancholy
until it mistakes the moon,
in its disguise, for the coveted
flaming pearl of wisdom.
the moon, depressed itself,
welcomes ministrations
from any quarter. the dragon
stretches out a limb to capture
the moon but lacks the aim,
the strength, the reach. just

as well, for the truth will out
when healing falls sway
to deception. the dragon
returns to its lair, head downcast.
the moon averts its eyes.

457

i search for more
but all that's left
in your features
are fossils
of moonlight
from the night
we almost kissed.

458

while you cowered
at my defiance, i could sleep
content but when you took on
the mantle of indifference,
i relented. now, my pleas
to you go unanswered
and i can only toss and turn.
you've waited me out.

459

apply a dab of cream
to the affected area
before bedtime
but no more
than will vanish
with a light swipe
and all will be limpid
by morning.

460

the moon is a serpent,
undulating, fluid, protean,
cunning, a hiss, a fog
of ambiguity, a wish
you wish would come
truly true.

461

it seemed you had betrayed me
by your absence but no,
you were giving me time
to reflect on nothingness.
i failed to appreciate
your resolution until you reappeared,
a wisp of yourself but overbrimming
with reassurance.

462

alright, i know i'd been encouraging
our trysts, but that time i was ready
to hit the hay, i needed a break,
some privacy. i thought you caught
my drift but was distressed to find you
burrowed in a fold of my comforter.
your hop-skipping when i fluffed
it up added insult to injury. i swore
i heard a chuckle from on high,
as if you were taking delight
in outsmarting me. but i can also play
that game. ergo i lowered the blinds.

463

i know you mean the best, my friend
but your feeble light won't do

the trick for the workaday affairs
at my doorstep calling out for clarity.
repair, instead, to the star-crossed
lovers. work your magic on them.

464

the moon is moving away, it's true,
an inch and a half a year
but in billions more, at least not soon,
it will find a sweet spot for orbiting,
drift no more and sing a different tune.

465

the moon does not divulge
its secrets, timing, or intent
when fading from my view
but letting out and reeling in
the line, i've learned enough
of what it holds, unfolds
and where it goes to know
it keeps me in its thoughts
and will be back when day is done.

466

even with intermittent recovery
night after night, it's disquieting,
this tabulation of all i've lost
from day to day.

467

i concede. i cannot vie
with your chaste whiteness,
circumscribed and proper.
i'm swarthy and uncurbed.
go ahead and tame me.
be quick about it and don't

let up your guard. a moment
out of your sight and i may
cower and take flight.

468

ultrathin, translucent, annular
slice of the giant turnip,
mockingly dares you to look
into rather than through
and taunts "go ahead,
just try to bite if you dare."

469

rampaging elephant, ears flapping,
trumpeting, clamorous advance,
raging, storms across borders
and barricades but gracefully
kneels at beck and call
of roadside traveler hailing
a ride, and shifts to peaceful gait
to carry and carry on.

470

glamour has abandoned you
just now in your gibbous garb.
despite your lack of stylish pose
and failure to evoke loving
feelings in the starry eyed,
i applaud your one-off bold
and independent stance,
this intermittent repudiation
of mere romance.

471

snatch! caught!
into the snuff bottle you go.

got you plugged up,
sealed, out of options.
now to slap an imposter
up there. who'd know
the difference or recognize
the shrunken prisoner
on my shelf?

472

generations have witnessed the gauzy,
cloud-draped moon, like a scrim-
projected phantom. history has taken note
of the theatrics of dreamy shifting
patterns abetting and subduing luster.

473

materializing out of nowhere,
the sudden, resplendent moon
defies my lack of expectations.

474

in preparation, the water boils
and bubbles. in one fell swoop,
a cup of jasmine rice dives in.
when foam dies down, the pot
is covered and set to simmer.
pervading the kitchen—a faint,
distant hum, real or imagined
but genuine enough to reckon with.

475

have you seen it? i was tossing
a spongy foam ball against the brick
back wall of a shuttered liquor store
and catching it on the rebound.

one time, as my concentration wavered,
i dropped it and the ball took off
with a mind of its own. i lost track
of it among the feet of unconcerned
pedestrians. please call number below
to arrange return. no questions asked.
you'll be well rewarded

476

on the roof's peak,
the black squirrel's
curved tail snared
what eluded you
everywhere else.

477

as reported by five Canterbury monks
in 1178, the crescent moon was like
a throbbing wounded snake and sudden
spitting flashes were widespread. tales
of lunar flares should not be brushed aside.

478

the desert, that's the place
to surrender to sky,
the desert at night,
to be willingly vanquished
by insomnia.

479

it's your brightness puts us to shame.
self-conscious of our dim deportment,
we contract, and rely on you to inform us
of ourselves. send love to poke us
out of hiding.

480

i'm stuck on the fantasy. never mind
it's a big rock, plain and simple
or that i'd suffocate there. i imbue
it with life no less plausible
than my own. who can fault me
for self-medicating on self-delusions?

481

all day long i wait
to pull in what
i'm guaranteed
to catch eventually.

all night long i hold
onto the false hope
that i won't
be left in the cold.

all i wish for
is my due
and not to lose
anything more.

482

served on a silver plate,
it's as much as i need
to survive. i give it
a healthy spin
and it takes to the rim.
i may harbor doubts
about never-ending
myths but in my heart
there are no contradictions.

483

it was hard reflection
in an illuminating night
that unwedged me
from the ravine of misery
and furnished me
with the confidence
to overturn the faulty
verdict i had reached
that i was better off alone.
i hurried back.

484

there is no solace in accepting that
the moon will be in its place
when you are not or that months
will continue to clock in.
your tears, remorsefully shed,
flood upward to trail its inexorable arc.

485

after immersion in the core
for what seems like forever,
you unearth the key to breaking
free, but you've come
by your wisdom too late
and prying off the lid
of confinement is an option
no more.

486

i'm nervous about the depth,
the endless tunnel of space,
the boundless space of time.
unfathomable, this dizzying

descent. i'm soothed by nods
of sympathetic assent and tokens
of assurance, geometric planes
positioned to intercept
my restive mind and keep it
from digging or reading too much
into temptation, and letting me stay
engaged, at least to start,
with the compliant surface.

487

bone china.
      i tilt
      my head back,
penetrate
      translucency
glide
along the edge,
      swim
      through deceptively
smooth surfaces,
saturated
      with illumination.

488

you kept wav(er)ing
      good (bye), bye (bye),
      in the car's rear-
view mirror. a mirage?
      i wondered, but
      returned your farewell
with a backward jiggle
      of my hand.
      at once
you were (far) gone
      or was it me,
      and i knew

how it felt
        to be wrong
        for so long.

489

alarms, sirens, warnings
        flashing,
        always someplace
far enough away
        you can't guess
        where
but in time
        enigmas
        will be resolved
and you'll be able
        to pinpoint to a degree
        unimaginable.

490

knots in the bridge's planks,
water lilies, yellow and pink
near the bank, a bellbird's
blaring call, and a sensation
in the concavity between
your shoulders, halfway
between pleasure and pain.
easy to predict what's next
on the agenda.

491

i made the mistake of inferring
that your five hundred defeats
branded you as defeated.
had i only put more stock
in you than in your outcomes,
i would not have lost the benefit
of your treasure trove of triumph.

492

Japanese quail feeding
on white millet and insects
concentrate on the ground
but their sixth sense
is mindful of another fortune
their bellies can't comprehend,
pronounced *tsuki* in Japan.

493

he jogged in the early hours,
steadily, consistently,
alongside the monotonous
parkway, opposite the flow
of oncoming traffic.
some regulars waved,
gave him a thumbs up
or momentarily flashed
their headlights. being
on the same wavelength—
that's what mattered most.

494

hopelessness is the changing
unchanging that shifts the context
of the contention but not its core
and leaves you at loose ends.

helplessness is the unchanging
changing that fits a formula
too shiftily stable for you
to be on firm ground.

absolute changing is being
unable to set foot.
absolute unchanging,
when you forever stay put.

495

what squadron did you say?
and that insignia on your uniform?
looks like an army of ants
crisscrossing a series of bridges.
what is your home planet?
where is the rest of your crew?
what led you to take this journey?

496

i forfeited
this evening's moon
not for anything
i did or said
but because i forgot
to pay it homage.
some excuses
are inexcusable.

497

i learned
my fractions
not by slicing
pies or sharing
pennies
but by taking lessons
from an exemplar
of continuity.

498

the adjacent soccer field
and baseball diamond
are empty, the children's
playground, childless.
a thrush starts to vocalize.
alone on the court, you shoot

hoops methodically, machine-
like, fixated not on the rim,
but a corner of the transparent
backboard, and amaze yourself
at how few bank shots you miss.

499

even in this obscure basement suite,
with outside views of little more
than legs parading, i am attuned
to your nearness by signals and clues,
unseen, unheard, unmistakable.

500

all day long i tried
to slow down
but you eclipsed me
at every juncture,
made me look
like a reckless
speed demon,
no matter my crawl.
let me hitch a ride.
teach me to match
your deliberate pace.

Postscript

"What more trite, hackneyed, worn out poetic image, metaphor or symbol than the moon. It's best to turn your back on it and shun it as its far side does to you. Ignore this stale excuse for wonders untold before you find yourself drowning in romantic and foolish poppycock, writing that is archaic, overdone and irrelevant at best."—Anonymous (or so he says)

$\mathbf{P}$hilip Wexler, originally from Brooklyn, New York, is a long-time resident of Bethesda, Maryland. He has had close to 200 poems published in magazines and privately dabbles in short fiction. His book-length poetry collections include *The Sad Parade* (prose poems) and *The Burning Moustache* (both from Adelaide Books), *The Lesser Light* (Finishing Line Press), and *I Would be the Purple* (Kelsay Books). He has organized several monthly spoken word series in the Washington, DC area, most recently *Words out Loud,* remotely since the onset of the coronavirus pandemic but with the hope of an eventual return to in-person events.

Phil's formal education includes the unlikely combination of undergraduate degrees in Math and English and a Master's in Library Science. Most of Phil's professional career has been with the U.S. federal government, specifically at the Toxicology and Environmental Health Information Program of the National Library of Medicine, part of the National Institutes of Health, from which he is now retired. He has written and edited many technical works bearing on toxicological sciences. He served as Editor-in-Chief of Elsevier's *Information Resources in Toxicology*, now in its 5th edition and has the same role in the 4th edition of its *Encyclopedia of Toxicology,* currently in progress, and the ongoing series, *History of Toxicology and Environmental Health.* He is also an editor of CRC Press' *Chemicals, Environment, Health: A Global Management Perspective* and the Taylor and Francis journal, *Global Security: Health, Science and Policy.* A long-time member of the U.S. Society of Toxicology, Phil is a recipient of its Public Communications Award and serves as a Trustee for the Toxicology Education Foundation.

In addition to literary (including simply reading) and technical writing pursuits, Phil is passionate about the arts, both in general and as a non-commercial mosaic artist, and frequents museums and galleries. He is also keen on music, particularly opera and Broadway musicals, and theatre. He has explored many other hobbies in the past which, if time were unlimited, he would still be engaged in. Among them were worldwide bicycle touring, hiking, fencing, bread-baking, woodworking, etc. Although his involvement in outdoor gardening has somewhat diminished, he still avidly tends to his houseplants, largely cacti and succulents, which thrive in a sunroom with southeastern exposure.

Phil relies heavily on *The Washington Post, Harper's,* and *The Atlantic* to keep him apprised of national and world news and commentary. He is increasingly concerned about political upheavals at home and abroad and the declining state of the global environment but tries to be hopeful about both. He is married to Nancy and helplessly dotes on their dog, Gigi. His son, Jake, and wife, Amanda, live nearby.

www.ingramcontent.com/pod-product-compliance
Lightning Source LLC
Chambersburg PA
CBHW021147090426
42740CB00008B/984